A Beginner's Guide to Controlling Your Anger

Table of Contents

A Beginners Guide to Controlling Your Anger.......1

Table of Contents.......2

Introduction.......3

Chapter 1: Reasons for Anger.......5

Chapter 2: Effects of Anger and Types of Anger.......12

Chapter 3: Techniques to Make Yourself Stay Calm.......17

Chapter 4: Simple tricks to curb anger........24

Chapter 5: Benefits of Having a Calm and Anger-free Life.......34

Conclusion.......38

Introduction

I want to thank you and congratulate you for purchasing the book *"A Beginners Guide to Controling Your Anger "*. This book contains proven steps and strategies on how to become a truly peaceful and calm person with a joyous and positive approach to life.

Here's an inescapable fact: you will need to know how your mind works and how anger affects the daily way of life. This book also helps you to cultivate simple anger management tricks that aids in curbing down anger for a calm and stress-free life. If you do not develop your ability to control the rage of anger, life is going to be tough for you and everyone around you. Controlling anger and staying calm is always important if you want to embrace the peace and serenity of everything good around you.

It's time for you to become an amazing person who is always calm and relaxed through the phase of life for the betterment of yourself and others in the society. This book lends a clear crystal view of anger and the drastic effects it can bring on a person. It also guides you on how to stay calm with simple psychological tricks that aid in curbing down anger for your own betterment and others around you.

Chapter 1: Reasons for Anger

Anger is an intense kind of emotion that is natural expression or reaction to certain experiences. The beginning phase of this emotion tends to grow from the few months of being born as a human. It is an integral part of all the motions that make us human. However, this emotion is healthy only if it is under control and when it gets out of control, it has the ability to inflict emotional and physical damages to yourself and people around you.

There are many reasons for a person to develop anger management issues and finally an outburst of anger. Anger is an emotion that can't be managed solely by controlling it all by yourself. It should be studied and the cause of anger should be identified to treat it accordingly. Some of the causes for anger management issues are as follows:

- **Witnessing anger and poor anger management while growing up:**

This seems to the most common way of developing anger management issues. Children who tend to witness angry outbursts from their parents in their childhood grow up by believing that venting out anger is acceptable and that there is nothing wrong in that. By watching parents or adults who react and express anger in a harsh way, they tend it translate the same expression in their life and they grow with a mind that it is perfectly alright to showcase the same emotion as a normal reaction.

- **Experience of abuse:** Children or adults who are abused in any way are at risks of developing an anger management issue. As they experience abuse and as they react to it, they grow up realizing that it is one of the effective and safest emotion to show when they are vulnerable to an abuse. And, sometimes if the abuse is too much, the brain chemistry changes and they find it hard to adjust to anger and other emotions. After a traumatic experience, a person is most likely to vent out his/her anger.

- **Stress mismanagement:** When stress is not handled properly, it leads to lowering of the limit of feeling overwhelmed. Stress because of a tiring job, a complicated relationship or a death of a loved one causes one to go over that threshold and they retaliate by venting out anger. This might cause the stress to last and it becomes chronic, which in turn leads to frequent anger outburst that is really bad for yourself and everyone around you. It becomes a habit for dealing with feelings of overwhelm and becomes a risky emotion to express.

- **Low self-esteem and low frustration tolerance:** For those who have a low self-esteem, misunderstanding of events and things as a threat to themselves and their goals are common. People like these, carry anger as an instinctive emotional reaction to a threat. This makes them to react to this misunderstood threat with the sole expression of anger. And everyone at some points in their lives gets to experience low frustration tolerance. For a few, this intolerance to frustration is not temporary and they find it hard to even handle moderate levels of frustration. Thus, a reaction to counter this intolerance is mostly a lash out of anger which is harmful for them and people around them.

- **Curbing and controlling emotions:** Some families want their kids not to express some emotions in front of anyone. This makes the children to think that they should not express these emotions in public and are not acceptable. They bottle it in and it results in building up of stress, which blows out all of a sudden resulting in a furious rage of anger. Expressing emotions are a necessity and they are an integral part of natural life, regardless of age and gender. Thus, curbing and controlling emotions are not really healthy and they might lead to poor anger management issues later.

- **Medications:** Certain medications have an ability to alter the way mind works and it results in numerous side effects. Overdosing of medication and taking in wrong medication can result in venting out of excessive anger. This is possible because it might lead a dangerous imbalance in the mind and the body that makes a person vulnerable. A person who is vulnerable in such cases looks to take the easiest and most effective form of expression to showcase the same, which is anger.

- **Lack of sleep:** Sleep is essential to have a balanced and healthy lifestyle.

When a sleep pattern is altered and when a person does not get enough sleep, he/she will start to develop an edgy feeling along with irritation. This causes temporary lashing out of anger. In other scenarios, people with chronic sleeping problems like insomnia, sleep apnea and other sleeping disorders are in risk of giving out recurrent bouts of anger.

- **Hiding emotions:** There are some emotions that are too hurting and overwhelming that they become hard to express. At these instances, people tend to overshadow them by expressing anger. Vulnerable are those who are under emotions such as hurt, sadness, loneliness or grief. They hide all these emotions and express anger just to feel safe. This kind of hiding and bottling up of emotions is clearly a bad way to get out of the problem. Any problem can be discussed and solutions can be sought for the same. That is why friends and family are there for. Asking them for emotional and mental support is nothing wrong and you will feel safe and secure when you say it all out to someone without hiding.

Discussed above are some of the most common causes and reasons for anger problems. However, each and everyone experience different and unique situations. The right way to control anger issues is to identify the cause of anger and learnt to control it to live a better and healthier life.

Chapter 2: Effects of Anger and Types of Anger

Types of anger: When dealing with anger, there are basically two types of anger. Passive anger and aggressive anger.

Passive anger is one of a kind and those who experience passive anger might not even realize that they are angry. Persons dealing with this kind tend to display their anger through sarcasm, apathy or meanness. They might also develop self-defeating habits such as bunking school/colleges or work, separating themselves from friends and family, and performing poorly in professional and social situations. For those around you, it might look like it is an intentional sabotaging, but they might not realize that it is hard for you to explain your actions.

Aggressive anger is another kind where the individual is aware of the emotion, but he/she might not be able to find the true roots of that behavior. This kind of anger tends to bring out really violent anger outbursts to counter or deal with real world problems. This form of anger is highly volatile and can result in damages physically and emotionally. Recognizing triggers and management of anger symptoms are necessary to deal with this kind of anger.

In another perspective anger can be categorized into several accepted forms such as:

- Chronic anger, which affects the immune system and causes mental disorders

- Passive anger, which is hard to identify and doesn't come across as anger

- Overwhelmed anger, caused by demands of life that becomes difficult for a person to cope up with

- Self-inflicted anger, caused by feelings of guilt

- Judgmental anger, which is directed to other people and comes with feelings of resentment

- Volatile anger, which comes with instant bouts of violent reactions

Effects of anger: When anger lasts for extended periods of time, it starts to become hard to deal with tiny aggravations in life. This will make it hard for you to de-stress. It can also affect your everyday activities including work. Effects of anger will make it hard for you to focus on any tasks and you will start becoming inefficient to accomplish projects. People will start to ignore you and they might not want to work alongside you. All this can lead to developing a feeling of guilt, remorse or shame.

If this kind of anger and stress lasts for long, you will also be unable to let loose, which is very critical for a good mental well-being. Excess of anger also affects the physical well-being at risk. Emotions are contagious and anger can affect the people in your life by casting a negative feeling when you are around them. This can cause them to feel let down, put off, intimidated, scared and scarred. The risk of running of loved ones from your life will also increase.

Anger explosions: Few people have very little control over their anger and they tend to explode in rage. This rage of anger can lead to physical abuse or violence. Thus, people with low self esteem fly into rages and utilize anger as a form to manipulate others and to feel powerful.

Anger repression: Some people on the other hand feel that anger is a bad and inappropriate emotion to choose. They tend to suppress it and this bottling up of emotions turn into depression and anxiety. Some might also vent this bottled emotion at innocent parties such as kids or pets which is riskier and harmful.

Few short term and long term health problems due to anger include headache, digestive problems, abdominal pain, insomnia, anxiety, depression, high blood pressure, heart attack and stroke.

Unresolved anger issues cause anxiety that have immediate effects such as dizziness, rapid breathing, nausea, muscle pain, muscle tension, headaches and troubles with concentration and memory. This can make it hard to do even routine tasks and can add up to the generalized anger about life. Long term anxiety can induce risk to physical and emotional well-being. People who are affected from long terms of anxiety have greater risks of strokes along with serious memory loss, sleep disorders and relationship issues.

Chapter 3: Techniques to Make Yourself Stay Calm

Being calm is not much of a Zen skill to acquire. It can be developed easily and this habit has the power to curb out all ill effects of anger. A calm mind and soul will have the perfect aura to take on the biggest of the troubles of lives. Reducing stress and being cool is as simple and requires just a balanced state of mind. By practicing a few of the below discussed things, a calm well being can be developed for your own good.

- Let go of the things and people that affect your emotional well-being. It is not the end of the world and stressing about a single situation is not going to do any good. If you are in those kinds of situations, just let it go.

- Breathing deeply is a proven method to de-stress and make yourself calm. Any stressful situation can be handled with just a minute of deep breathing. Five deep breaths in and out of the body along with an imagination of stress leaving your body through every exhale can do wonders.

- Loosen up your body physically and perform an instant body scan to find the areas that are tight and tense. A clenched jaw or rounded shoulders can be loosened up by a gentle touch or massage.

- Look at your dining etiquette and chew slowly. Learn patience and also lose weight by chewing down the food slowly. Pay attention to the taste, texture and flavor of every dish. This habit of chewing slowly can directly induce a sense of patience in you.

- While going after a bold and tough goal, always approach it with patience as it requires the same. Do not start focusing on the end result. Give yourself consistent positive feedback and grow your patience. Stay happy and embrace the journey of life. It is okay to have a deeper perspective in life. But the same thing gets tricky if you dig in deep into any problem. Learn to adapt to the situation accordingly and find ways to achieve something tough. Always have hope that there are many ways to get things done and if one of them doesn't work, there are many more to try.

- If your stress levels are skyrocketing the next time, take a deep breath and ask yourself if it is going to matter in a couple of days. Most of the things that stresses you wouldn't even matter the very next week. Stop raging over the things that you can't control and stop hurting yourself and others around you for the same.

- Remember that no one is perfect. Do not demand perfection to yourself as it might stress you out. Learn to be patient and calm with who you are and accept that you can't be perfect. This acceptance can lead to a deeper sense of understanding of yourself.

- Practice patience every day. A simple practice of patience can enhance your ability to remain calm and cool in the face of stress and anger. Get in the longest line in a store; go inside a bank instead of opting a drive-thru and take long walks through a secluded park.

- The best way to manage stress and anger is to look for the signs in the first place and stop that from building up. It might be hard to identify the danger zone, but signals from the body can be subtle like lack of sleep and frequent headaches. Catch on these signals and try to pluck the weed out in the beginning.

- Change and alter your focus if you are stressed or angry. When you feel tense, you might get the urge to mentally find out what went wrong. Find a quiet place to sit down and shift your focus to your body instead.

- Do not use stress as an excuse to skip your daily exercise. Working out helps to bring a balance in stress hormones. Take a break by walking up and down flights of stairs, sign up for a boxing class, dance with some mellow music and experiment stuff that you loved and always wanted to do.

- Eat right and avoid sugary munchies. They increase the blood-glucose level and make you feel jittery. Dip fresh strawberries in dark chocolate sauce and enjoy a beneficial bite to decrease stress hormones. Also opt for carrots or celery sticks that produce crunchy sounds to help release pent-up frustration. The right diet can do wonders to your body and mind.

- Call a friend and spend time with your closed ones. Meet a friend if you are really stressed or angry and tell him/her your whole situation. Just letting out of things can help in reducing the burden in your heart.

- Don't be stuck in the same place when you are at risk of stress and anger. Go out and breathe some fresh air to refresh your body and mind. Embrace a head-clearing moment by walking in a garden. Behold and smell the aura of flowers and leaves to reduce the stress hormone levels.

- It is also normal that all your worries and stress build up in your head just before you go to bed. So prepare yourself for the bed and reach for a pad and pen to write down all the negative thoughts in your mind. Lack of sleep can make you more anxious, so it is better to have a healthy sleeping cycle.

- Find the source of your stress before fighting it. Identity the cause of this emotion and try to curb it in the beginning. It is easier said than done, but for every individual this source of stress changes and only you can figure out what is bothering you. If the source is found out and if steps are taken to curb stress and anger in the beginning, life will become much easier for you and others around you.

Chapter 4: Simple tricks to curb anger

Anger is quite easy to cut down with just some simple tricks to follow. Being a state of mind and a reactive emotion, it can be curbed with a little effort. There are many ways to manage anger and few of those are listed briefly below:

Think before you let out words: Words are let out quite easily at the heat of any moment. Losing temper more often easily makes you yell out words without even thinking. And later it becomes something you regret. So, it is essential that you control the way you speak and express yourself. Take a brief moment inside your mind to collect your thoughts. Allow other people involved in the situation to do the same. Then react after a while and this can lead to a solution that is favorable to everyone involved in the situation. So, always take care of the words that you vent out in fury and anger. This way you can free yourself from a guilt-trip full of regrets.

Express your anger only when you are calm: Always express your anger and emotion in an assertive way that is non-confrontational. Put down the concerns and needs directly, neatly and clearly. Make sure that you do not hurt others when you express the same. It is also good if you do not control them while expressing the anger. This way of expression comes after a lot of thinking process and it is the best way to put an end to the situation that has been created.

Take a break and workout: Stress takes a toll on the physical state as well as mental state. Physical activities help in decreasing the stress level that causes anger. If your anger shows no sign of reduction, go out of the scenario. Take a brisk and fresh walk or run immediately. Do something that you love to do alone and enjoy the physical change it delivers. This is also a healthy way to ignore a source of anger in the beginning.

Do not feel bad to take a timeout: Timeouts and intervals are not only for kids, they are effective for adults too. Make sure that you give yourself short breaks during a tough day at work. Do not let the work take a toll on your stress level. Enjoy a few moments of quiet time alone and always be prepared to handle what is coming next. Also, assure that you do not get irritated or angry easily.

Find out possible solutions: There are times when situations go out of hand and make you go mad. In those times, instead of focusing on what made you made, try to focus on solving the issue at hand. Always remember that anger does not fix anything and it only makes things worse. There are solutions to every problem and make sure that you always recognize the problem and come up with a decent solution for the same. Discuss with the people involved to get a solution that works for everyone involved in the situation. Finding out possible situations for a problem and optimizing the best solution for the same by considering every individual's opinion is a healthy way to settle any dispute. This way, you will always be respected in that circle.

Follow "I" statements: To avoid making someone feel criticized or blamed, use "I" statements to express the problem. Instead on putting the blame on them, use a specific kind of statement that express that you are upset or insulted because of such behavior from them. For example, say "I'm upset that you didn't take the clothes off from the dryer", instead of saying that, "You never do any housework". This way, the person involved in the situation will start feeling guilty without being criticized or blamed.

Do not hold a grudge for longer: "To err is humane, to forgive is divine". Forgiving someone is a great way to break down the problem. It is a powerful tool that brings in more love and joy instead of hatred and rage. Allowing anger and other negative emotions to crowd out positive vibes leads to a bitter sense of injustice.

Use comedy and humor to de-stress and release tension: Tension can be effortlessly reduced by lightening up in a state of mind. If you're faced with something that makes you angry, use humor to help you face it in the most jovial way possible. This does not mean that you should choose sarcasm to express the emotion. Sarcasm has the ability to hurt other's feelings and that can make things worse. Find something funny and positive in every problem that you face. This can lead to an irritation-less perspective of life and problems in life.

Practice relaxation skills: When anger reaches the epitome of its point, relax yourself and put that to vent out the rage and fury. Follow deep-breathing exercises and practice yoga to indulge yourself in a calm state of being. Imagine a relaxing scene or place whenever you are stressed out. Repeat a calming word or phrase like "take it easy", "everything is going to be alright" and so on. Listening to your favorite music is also a nice way to calm down. Indulge in the habit of journals and write down day to day happenings.

Seek help only when it is a necessity: Controlling anger is a challenge by itself for everyone at times. Regular seeking of help for anger issues is not healthy and you should learn when to seek help. Ask for help from someone only if it gets out of control. You are in the risk of venting out the angry bout when you seek help. This might cause you to do or say things that you might regret later.

There are many other healthy ways to vent out your anger that works for all:

1. Use words and translate your anger into words to share with someone you trust completely. This helps in providing a balance in both physical and emotional state. Express in subtle ways that do not harm or make the other person involved in the situation to get angry. This is one of the healthiest ways of expressing the anger you have. Use of words to express anger also improves the creativity in you.

2. Put your problems in writing and share it with your loved ones so that they will understand the situation you are in. Face to face conversations can lead to trouble when you are angry. Journaling about stressful events also help in strengthening the immune system and reduce the stress levels in the body.

3. Hit something that does not break or tear on hitting. Hit or scream into a pillow instead of reacting at a person. This helps in stabilizing feelings when things are gone mad. But, this should also be done in limits. If you are punching a pillow, do it only for 30 seconds a time. Running in a treadmill fast also helps. Habit of walking daily in the morning relaxes the mind and helps to control anger. Walking also helps in decreasing diastolic blood pressure.

4. Cognitive restructuring means the altering the way you think. Thinking while angry can get more dramatic. There are some strategies under this to control anger:

- **Avoid usage of words like "never" or "always":** Do not use statements like "This never succeeds" or "You are always ruining the plan. These statements make you feel that your anger is justified and there is no solution to the problem. These also alienate and insult the people who you intend them to.

- **Focus on goals:** Think of what you want to achieve and then state the problem that you might face. Try to find a solution to that specific problem that hinders you from reaching the goal.

- **Use logic:** Even justified anger tends to become irrational. Always remember that the world is not against you and this is just a phase of rough time. Repeat this in your mind each time and get through tough times with better perspective.

- **Change expectations into desires:** Do not demand things. Do not let your disappointment turn into anger. Some of you use anger to avoid feeling hurt but really that doesn't make the hurt go away. Change your demands into humble requests. Say that you would like it rather than saying that you must have it.

Chapter 5: Benefits of Having a Calm and Anger-free Life

Overcoming anger and staying calm is a virtue to possess. The state of blissful calmness and serenity in being can lead to a fantastic change in physical, emotional and spiritual well-being. Changes in all these forms of your life tend bring in a change in the way you affect everyone around you. With all positivity in your calm mind, you will reach the epitome of your conscious self and you will start believing in yourself to achieve the heights that you want to conquer.

Being calm brings in a peace of mind called as inner peace which has various numbers of benefits:

- Your ability to concentrate will increase abundantly and you will able to focus on a thing in hand and come up with a solution to any problem with a calm peace of mind.

- Your daily affairs of life will be handled with much efficiency to your own surprise. You will automatically come up with a good way to handle your every day.

- A sense of inner strength and power will arise giving way to an active and optimistic mindset that is designed to achieve every little thing that you desire.

- The mere sensation of freedom from the effects of stress, anxieties and worries is a big plus in staying calm and peaceful. Life will be much easier and you will always face the most difficult situations with a positive approach to succeed.

- You will start feeling happy and blissful on the inside and life will become joyous. You will carry a positive aura that attracts other people towards you.

- Sleep is a hard thing to get when you are stressed and angry. When you have a peaceful state of mind, you will be able to fall asleep easily and you will enjoy a sound and cozy slumber throughout the night.

- Your physical and mental well-being will be perfect with a fit and active mind that is ready to take on challenges put forth.

With a calm and relaxed mind, you can easily take control of your life. You will start to develop trust and faith within the self and others. Focus and clarity in vision of your goals will be increased along with a vibrant health both emotionally and physically. With positive energy and good mental concentration, your creative juice will flow in the right directions. The sense of self-awareness will increase and you will be able to master the subconscious mind. By connecting with your heart, you will develop great intuition with an enhanced equilibrium. Body and mind will be cleansed and your healing potential will be increased for your own good and others around you.

All this will lead you to live a life joyfully with higher levels of awareness. This kind of versatile flexibility in mind and body will make your presence powerful and positive in any situation. You will be able to transform negativity and bring in more balance to life. By gaining clarity and insight, you will be able to make effective decisions that will change the course of your life drastically in a good way. Thus, you can become the master of your own destiny and lead a healthy life ahead in all forms of life. You will succeed both financially and spiritually with a wider perspective to problems and their solutions.

Conclusion

Thank you again for purchasing this book!

I hope this book was able to help you to teach you all about anger and effects of anger. Anger can be controlled and a state of calm well-being can be put into practice to indulge yourself in a healthy and active lifestyle. After looking at all the benefits of having a calm and relaxed mind, you might as well start considering a change in the way you approach life and problems in life.

The next step is to follow the simple steps to control your anger. Rage and fury for every little thing is unhealthy and it is high time you realize the same. These techniques are proven methods to indulge in a calm well-being that is good for you and others around you.

Finally, if you enjoyed this book, please take the time to share your thoughts and post a review on Amazon. It'd be greatly appreciated!

Thank you and good luck!

Printed in Great Britain
by Amazon